G000153712

This edition copyright
© 2000 Lion Publishing
Illustrations copyright
© 2000 David Holmes
Published by
Lion Publishing plc
Sandy Lane West,
Oxford, England
www.lion-publishing.co.uk
ISBN 0 7459 4224 5
First edition 2000
10 9 8 7 6 5 4 3 2

A catalogue record for this
book is available from the
British Library
Typeset in 11/15
Elegant Garamond
**Printed and bound in China
by Imago**

Acknowledgments

15, 42, 61: I Corinthians 13:4–7,
Song of Songs 1:15, 2:2, Isaiah
54:10, quoted from the Good
News Bible published by The
Bible Societies/HarperCollins
Publishers Ltd, UK © American
Bible Society 1966, 1971, 1976,
1992, used with permission.
58–59: 'One Perfect Rose',
copyright 1926, renewed
1954 by Dorothy Parker, from
The Portable Dorothy Parker
by Dorothy Parker. Used by
permission of Viking Penguin,
a division of Penguin Putnam
Inc., and of Gerald Duckworth
& Co. Ltd. Every effort has been
made to trace and acknowledge
copyright holders of all the
quotations in this book. We
apologize for any errors or
omissions that may remain, and
would ask those concerned to
contact the publishers, who will
ensure that full acknowledgment
is made in the future.

To my love

Compiled by Sarah Hall

LION
Giftlines

This thing called love

'Love' can mean many different
things. That peculiar feeling
in the stomach when a
certain person approaches.
Despairing admiration
for someone amazing but
quite out of reach. Relief
and a feeling of safety when the
one truly reliable person turns up…

Here's a collection of thoughts about love from several different angles — even the cynics get a look-in. But God gets the last word. After all, God invented love.

What is
This Thing?

The Eskimos had fifty-two
names for snow because
it was important to them: there
ought to be as many for love.

MARGARET ATWOOD

The desire of the moth for the star,
  Of the night for the morrow,
The devotion to something afar
From the sphere of our sorrow.

PERCY BYSSHE SHELLEY

*I*t is only with the heart that one
can see rightly; what is essential
is invisible to the eye.

ANTOINE DE SAINT-EXUPÉRY

L ove seeks only one thing: the good of the one loved. It leaves all the other secondary effects to take care of themselves. Love, therefore, is its own reward.

THOMAS MERTON

L*ove is wanting to do what you don't want to do because you want to.*

MIKE YACONELLI

Love is patient and kind; it is not jealous or conceited or proud; love is not ill-mannered or selfish or irritable; love does not keep a record of wrongs; love is not happy with evil, but is happy with the truth. Love never gives up; and its faith, hope, and patience never fail.

FROM THE NEW TESTAMENT
FIRST LETTER TO THE CORINTHIANS

Love is more than words, but it is saying the words 'I love you.' Every day. Speaking them. Writing them. Singing them. Dancing them. Reading them. The words 'I love you' have a power all in themselves. The day you stop saying 'I love you' is the day your love starts to die.

MIKE YACONELLI

Immature love says: 'I love you because I need you.' Mature love says: 'I need you because I love you.'

ERICH FROMM

L ove is a choice: not simply, or
  necessarily, a rational choice,
but rather a willingness to be present
to others without pretence or guile.

CARTER HEYWARD

We only deliberately waste time
with those we love – it is the
purest sign that we love someone if
we choose to spend time idly in their
presence when we could be doing
something more constructive.

SHEILA CASSIDY

B eing in love is extraordinary because it has everything: pain, strength, patience, silence, happiness – extreme happiness, energy… and yet at the same time, it is so light that it has nothing!

JOHNNI POWELL

I want to feel love without making myself vulnerable. I also want to fly and not have to leave the ground.

K. BRADFORD BROWN

O*ne word
Frees us of all the weight
and pain of life:
That word is love.*

SOPHOCLES

Keep love in your heart. A life without it is like a sunless garden when the flowers are dead. The consciousness of loving and being loved brings a warmth and richness to life that nothing else can bring.

OSCAR WILDE

Heart
and soul

I cannot fix on the hour, or the spot, or the look, or the words, which laid the foundation. It is too long ago. I was in the middle before I knew I had begun.

JANE AUSTEN

B ut to see her was to love her,
love but her and love for ever.

ROBERT BURNS

O mistress mine, where are you
   roaming?
O, stay and hear! your true love's
   coming,
That can sing both high and low:
Trip no further, pretty sweeting;
Journeys end in lovers meeting,
Every wise man's son doth know.

WILLIAM SHAKESPEARE

W e talk, I believe, all day long:
to talk to each other is but a
more animated and an audible thinking.

CHARLOTTE BRONTË

*S*hall I compare thee
to a summer's day?
Thou art more lovely
and more temperate.

WILLIAM SHAKESPEARE

O, my Luve's like a red, red rose
That's newly sprung in June:
O, my Luve's like the melodie
That's sweetly play'd in tune!
As fair art thou, my bonnie lass,
So deep in luve am I:
And I will luve thee still, my dear,
Till a' the seas gang dry.

ROBERT BURNS

She walks in beauty, like the night
Of cloudless climes and starry skies;
And all that's best of dark and bright
Meet in her aspect and her eyes.

LORD BYRON

The music had the heat of blood,
  A passion that no words can reach;
We sat together, and understood
Our own heart's speech.
We had no need of word or sign,
The music spoke for us, and said
All that her eyes could read in mine
Or mine in hers had read.

ARTHUR SYMONS

I*f thou must love me, let it be for naught*
Except for love's sake only.

ELIZABETH BARRETT BROWNING

Doubt thou the stars are fire;
  Doubt that the sun doth move;
Doubt truth to be a liar;
But never doubt I love.

WILLIAM SHAKESPEARE

H e's *more myself than I am.*
Whatever our souls are made of,
his and mine are the same.

EMILY BRONTÉ

My bounty is as boundless as the sea,
My love as deep; the more I give
to thee,
The more I have, for both are infinite.

WILLIAM SHAKESPEARE

You are my only love. You have
me completely in your power.

JAMES JOYCE

My soul is so knit to yours that it is but a divided life I live without you. And this moment, now you are with me, and I feel that our hearts are filled with the same love, I have a fullness of strength to bear and do our Heavenly Father's will, that I had lost before.

GEORGE ELIOT

Getting Physical

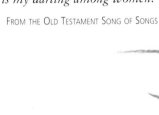

How beautiful you are,
   my love;
 how your eyes
shine with love!
Like a lily among thorns
   is my darling among women.

FROM THE OLD TESTAMENT SONG OF SONGS

*S*ee! how she leans her cheek
  upon her hand:
O! that I were a glove upon that hand,
That I might touch that cheek.

WILLIAM SHAKESPEARE

Jenny kiss'd me when we met,
    Jumping from the chair she sat in;
Time, you thief, who love to get
Sweets into your list, put that in!

Say I'm weary, say I'm sad,
Say that health and wealth
    have miss'd me,
Say I'm growing old, but add,
Jenny kiss'd me.

LEIGH HUNT

*Oh, they loved dearly: their souls
kissed, they kissed with their eyes,
they were both but one single kiss.*

HEINRICH HEINE

And the sunlight clasps the earth,
    And the moonbeams kiss the sea —
What are all these kissings worth,
If thou kiss not me?

PERCY BYSSHE SHELLEY

G*ive me a thousand kisses, then a hundred, then a thousand more.*

CATULLUS

Y ou cannot give
a kiss without
taking and cannot
take without giving.

*C*herry-ripe, ripe, ripe, I cry,
  Full and fair ones; come and buy.
If so be you ask me where
They do grow, I answer: There

Where my Julia's lips do smile;
There's the land, or cherry-isle,
Whose plantations fully show
All the year where cherries grow.

ROBERT HERRICK

When the gorse is out of bloom,
kissing's out of fashion.

ENGLISH PROVERB

Y ou are always new.
The last of your kisses
was ever the sweetest.

JOHN KEATS

Cynics' Corner

Falling in love consists merely in uncorking the imagination and bottling the common sense.

HELEN ROWLAND

If somebody says 'I love you,' to me, I feel as though I had a pistol pointed at my head. What can anybody reply under such conditions but that which the pistol-holder requires? — 'I love you, too.'

KURT VONNEGUT

A single flow'r he sent me,
 since we met.
All tenderly his
 messenger he chose;
Deep-hearted, pure,
 with scented dew
 still wet –
One perfect rose.

O*ut upon it,*
I have loved
Three whole days together;
And am like to love three more,
If it prove fair weather.

SIR JOHN SUCKLING

Why is it no one ever sent me yet
One perfect limousine, do you suppose?
Ah no, it's always just my luck to get
One perfect rose.

DOROTHY PARKER

God says:
The mountains
and hills may crumble, but my
love for you will never end.

FROM THE OLD TESTAMENT BOOK OF ISAIAH